Simplifying Regular Expression Using Python
Learn Regular Expression like Never Before

A book by

Abhishek Singh (Data Scientist, M. Tech, B.E.)
Asst. Prof., Electronics and Communication Engineering Department,
Global Nature Care Sangathan Group of Institutions, Jabalpur

And

Zohaib Hasan (M. Tech, B.E.)
Asst. Prof., Electronics and Communication Engineering Department,
Global Nature Care Sangathan Group of Institutions, Jabalpur

Imprint: Independently Published
ISBN: 9781094777979
Edition: 1ˢᵗ **Ed.**
First print: May 2019

Statutory Warning

Contact:
Email ID: abhisheksingh@ggits.org
               zohaibhasan@ggits.org

Preface

Regular Expression is...

This has to be the ideal way to start the preface with. But I will start this topic in the chapter inside the book when I'll talk about Regular Expression.

Now the first thought which must be coming into everybody's mind is that: Oh no! Yet another book on Regular Expression. Then, a pool of questions: Why did the author choose this topic? What's new in this book? Is it useful for me? If yes, then, to what extent?

The second thought (which is appreciable, thank you), ok, let's give this guy a chance and read his work.

To begin with, yes, this is another book on Regular Expression. Why? To be honest, there are not many books on this topic as there should have been with due course of time. An additional fact is that there are not many books on Regular Expression using Python. This topic, for some reason, didn't get that name and fame as it should have been. When I was learning Python and became saturated after learning regular stuff, (although I had started Image Processing and Data Analysis, in parts) one of my colleagues, (who also happened to be the co-author of this book), suggested I try some string validations.

It was only then that I got into the powerful world of RegEx as Regular Expression is popularly called. And it was then when I (we) decided to write a book on this topic so that I can present maximum topics in one place collectively and to write the do's and don'ts that must be taken care of while programming.

Why did I choose Python as the base language? Python is very easy to learn even for newbies. There are numerous books on Python plus online help. Anyone can learn Python to an elementary level in a record time. I learned it in 7 days (with zero knowledge of any other programming language).

Who should read this book?

Well, this book is for the absolute beginners. The only prerequisite is elementary knowledge of Python. If you are new to this concept, this book is highly recommended irrespective of the engineering branch you belong to. If you are a bit familiar, then you can enhance yours as well as my knowledge.

I am an Electronics and Communication Engineer. Should I learn it? I am not a Computer Science Engineering guy. Why should I learn this thing?

The answer is that if Raspberry Pie (an electronic device) needs Python (a programming language) to complete itself, why I can't learn something to complete my knowledge.

Summary: *Beginners*- you are welcome to gain something new in the easiest method possible. *Professionals*- you are welcome to appreciate or criticize and help me improve my work.

How this book is arranged?

The book is designed to learn RegEx in a stress freeway. It is divided into 7 chapters which represent 7 days excluding a chapter on Introduction to RegEx. The ultimate aim is to learn RegEx in 7 days. Can I learn something in 7 days? Only 7 days. Seriously? Yes, you can learn even Chinese in 7 days. But, the key is to practice things to remember and master. The content summary goes like this:

Chapter 1 is the introduction of regular expression and *re* module

Chapter 2 or Day 1 is getting into some basic operations of regular expression and writing our 1st program.

Chapter 3 or Day 2 is doing some string manipulation using regular expression. This chapter will give an idea of what the concept of RegEx is capable of performing.

Chapter 4 or Day 3 is dedicated to password matching and validation with step by step analysis.

Chapter 5 or Day 4 is dedicated to a user ID or Login ID matching and validation with step-by-step analysis.

Chapter 6 or Day 5 is dedicated to email ID matching and validation with step-by-step analysis.

Chapter 7 or Day 6 is dedicated to some miscellaneous topics such as debit or credit card number, date of birth, etc. matching and validation with step-by-step analysis.

Chapter 8 or Day 7 is dedicated to some more applications of RegEx other than string matching and validation with step-by-step analysis. This chapter can be thought of as an extension to Chapter 3.

Every chapter is provided with detailed explanation of the content. Dedicated chapters have been provided for password validation, email ID validation, etc. And a point comes where *much explanation* becomes *self-explanation.* At this point, you'll be able to write any RegEx syntax on your own. The presentation of chapters is one of a kind.

Acknowledgment

First, thank the Almighty GOD for keeping me focused and keep enlightening my path to reach my goal.

A big thanks to my colleague, helping hand, and co-author of this book Zohaib Hasan, for introducing me to the concept of Regular Expression, for helping me to improve my logic while writing and understanding the codes, and for writing a few chapters and sharing his knowledge.
I am also thankful to my wife for her patience with which she motivated me to work hard day and night.

Lastly, I am thankful to every person and resource available (especially those provided by Amazon) who in direct or indirect ways helped me to complete this book.

Sincerely Yours,
Abhishek Singh

Dedicated to Anika, Zafeer
And
The wonderful branch
Of
Electronics and Communication Engineering

Table of Content

Introduction to Regular Expression

1.1 Regular Expression

A RegEx, or Regular Expression, is a sequence of characters that determines a search pattern. RegEx can be used to check if a string contains the specified search pattern. Along with this, RegEx also provides various operations for string manipulations such as validating an email or password or even extracting some data.

1.2 How useful Regular Expression is to learn?

Every popular language, like C, Java, Perl, Python, etc. supports Regular Expression. But unfortunately, Regular Expression does not earn that name and fame with the time that it should have been, providing the features and advantages it offers. Let's jot down some of them:

1. With writing a few characters, a lot can be achieved which otherwise, would have taken dozens of lines of codes.
2. As I already told you, unfortunately, RegEx did not become popular as it should have been, mostly because, many programmers don't know RegEx (ironically, but that's true). So, learning RegEx will give you a distinguished recognition.
3. Usage of a few characters means a faster execution time.
4. Perhaps one of the most important features is **Portability.** The majority of RegEx syntax works the same way in a variety of programming languages. So, learning one will make it easier to understand any other programming language's RegEx.

I am starting Regular Expression for Python Language. My love for Python is the foremost reason for selecting this language. And also, unarguably (or arguably maybe) Python is the easiest language of all to learn in a short period.

So, to begin our journey towards this course, the only prerequisite is some basic knowledge of normal python programming. **Yup!!** You read it correctly, *some basic knowledge of normal python programming.* And I mean this line. You don't need any sci-fi or rocket science knowledge of python (no prior knowledge of image processing, data processing, etc.) to dive into the ocean of Regular Expression.

1.3 Which tool or platform to use?

That's not a tricky part if you are already familiar with Python. I am using Jupyter Notebook via Anaconda on Windows 8. But you can use any IDE you like.

So, with this, we are ready to start our little journey.

Wait!! One minute...

What is the application of learning this *not-so-famous* thing? Do any fascinating names such as Google, Microsoft, etc. use this? What's the job prospect?

The answer is: Yes if you are a good RegEx programmer, you have great chances of getting absorbed by many dream companies. A simple example is Password and Email-ID validation of any login page of any Banking Website. Everybody needs a strong password. It's a simple application of RegEx (we will also learn to make a strong password in our journey).

RegEx is also used in web scraping, data wrangling, used for text matching in spreadsheets, text editors, IDEs, and Google Analytics.

So, let's ride the tide...

1.4 RegEx Module

Python has a built-in package called *re*, which can be used to work with Regular Expressions. Remember one thing, writing regular expression is an art. Like in VLSI, choosing process parameters is an art irrespective of the technology being used. Similarly, writing RegEx and applying it correctly needs art. The first step is to import this module by using the following line:

1st line of code: import re

Before starting the actual programming it's always a better approach to compile (or you can say pre-compile).

2nd line of code: pattern = re.compile (r"""")

The purpose of this step is to compile the RegEx pattern (pattern is a variable name) which will be used for matching later, and, although one can skip this step, but, believe me, it's really handy to compile RegEx when it'll be used several times in your program.

Hey!! What's this (r""")?

It's a prefix. Prefixing with an r simply indicates to the string that whatever we are writing inside double quotes should be treated literally and not as escape characters for python. **For example:**

print ("\n") will give an output as cursor blinking on the new line, but,

print (r"\n") will give an output as \n.

So, let's not skip the 2nd line of code while learning regular expression, and this means that the above two lines are mandatory before getting into the coding logic.

What should be our approach? The traditional way of 1st learning every data type, function, bla...bla...bla...all in a single run and then use it in examples or learn through examples at run time. I prefer the second approach and it's not boring also.

Day 1: Our 1st Program

2.1 The first program:

#Task 1 (Day 1): Ok!! Our 1st task is to **write a program that will replace all the digits in a string with an underscore (_)**

Let's talk about this task now. What should be the algorithm for this?

1. Input a string. The string should have digits also.

2. Find out the digits and replace them with an underscore.

3. Print the new string with an underscore.

Let's code it:

```
import re
pattern = re.compile(r"")
my_string = input("Enter a string: ")
pattern = re.compile(r"[0-9]+")
result = pattern.sub("_",my_string)
print(result)
```

Wow!! It took 6 lines only. Yup, that's the magic of using regular expression.

Let's do a postmortem of this code now.

1st two lines of codes are mandatory lines that we have discussed earlier. Again a reminder, 2nd line is not compulsory to write, but, it's a good practice.

3rd line of code: my_string = input ("Enter a string: ")

my_string is a variable in which the user is being asked to enter any string at run time.

5th line of code: result = pattern.sub ("_",my_string)

Again the **result** is a variable that is used to store the final result. In this final result, our input that is, my_string will be checked for a pattern, which is defined in the **4th line of code** (which we will analyze in a moment). By replacing, we can also say that we want to **substitute.** RegEx provides a **sub-function** that does the **substitution** part. The meaning of this line of code goes like this:

Substitute an underscore in my_string by checking the pattern, where pattern consists of digits.

"Pattern consists of digits" is described in the 4th line of code and that is the heart of the code. It is the 1st proper RegEx function to deal with.

4th line of code: pattern = re.compile (r"[0-9]+")

Here comes the 1st learning part of RegEx. What is this ([0-9]+)? The 1st table to learn is:

Table 1: Special Sequences

Element	Description
.	Matches any single character except newline character.
\d	This matches any digit [0-9]
\D	This matches non-digit characters [^0-9]
\s	This matches whitespace character [\t\n\r\f\v]
\S	This matches non-whitespace character [^ \t\n\r\f\v]
\w	This matches alphanumeric character [a-zA-Z0-9_]
\W	This matches any non-alphanumeric character [^a-zA-Z0-9_]
\A	Returns a match if the specified characters are at the beginning of the string
\b	Returns a match where the specified characters are at the beginning or the end of a word
\B	Returns a match where the specified characters are present, but NOT at the beginning (or the end) of a word
\Z	Returns a match if the specified characters are at the end of the string

There is nothing to panic about. We will only refer to this table when needed and by referring only we are going to memorize it. That's damn true…

Coming to our **4th line of code**, [0-9] will check for any digits starting from 0 to 9. Let's check the output now of our code:

```
import re
pattern = re.compile(r"")
my_string = input("Enter a string: ")
pattern = re.compile(r"[0-9]")
result = pattern.sub("_",my_string)
print(result)

Enter a string: john123
john___
```

So, the input string john123 after execution of code gives an output john___

Is there any difference with the code that was written earlier? Yes, one difference. ([0-9]+) v/s ([0-9]). What does this '+' sign do?

```
import re
pattern = re.compile(r"")
my_string = input("Enter a string: ")
pattern = re.compile(r"[0-9]+")
result = pattern.sub("_",my_string)
print(result)

Enter a string: john123
john_
```

Observe the change. Without '+' the output has as many underscores as many digits in the string. But after using '+' it's a single underscore.
The question is: What's the use?
'+' is used when a character is repeated one or more times. Using '+' **123** is treated as a single character. So, a single underscore is used. Without '+' **123** is treated as **1, 2, and 3** so, 3 underscores are used to represent 3 digits.

Again, as an art of writing, it is very useful when we do password validation. Actually, without '+' an intruder comes to know that how many digits are there and he/she/they can try for various permutations and combinations to break the password. '+'increase the security.

6th line of code: print (result)

This will finally print the result.
Let's refer to **Table 1** again. **[0-9]** can also be replaced with **\d**. Will it give the same result?

```
import re
pattern = re.compile(r"")
my_string = input("Enter a string: ")
pattern = re.compile(r"\d+")
result = pattern.sub("_",my_string)
print(result)
```

```
Enter a string: jason123
jason_
```

It works cool!!!

Let's do 1 more check. Can I write digits anywhere or it should be written continuously.

```
import re
pattern = re.compile(r"")
my_string = input("Enter a string: ")
pattern = re.compile(r"[0-9]+")
result = pattern.sub("_",my_string)
print(result)
```

```
Enter a string: 123jason456
_jason_
```

Ok. So, we can write digits in any manner. It will be substituted by an underscore.

Congratulations!! That's our 1st RegEx program and it's successful (and it's not the Hello World program).

#Task 2 (Day 1): One more example with **sub** will help to understand substitution function as well. Here, we are substituting digits with a **$** sign.

```
import re
pattern = re.compile(r"")
my_string = input("Enter a string: ")
pattern = re.compile(r"\d+")
result = pattern.sub("$",my_string)
print(result)
```

```
Enter a string: 2fast2furious
$fast$furious
```

So on Day 1, we have learned two functions: **sub** and **digits**.

Moving on, we used '+'. Does it have any name? **Yes.** It is known as a **Quantifier**. Quantifiers simply specify the number of characters to match. This brings us to **Table 2**. Again, there is no need to memorize it. We will learn it eventually like \d and **sub**.

Table 2: Quantifiers

Quantifier	Description	Example	Sample match
+	one or more	\w+	ABCDEF097
{2}	exactly 2 times	\d{2}	01
{1,}	one or more times	\w{1,}	smiling
{2,4}	2, 3 or 4 times	\w{2,4}	1234
*	0 or more times	A*B	AAAAB

| ? | once or none | \d+? | 1 in 12345 |

A set is a set of characters inside a pair of square brackets [] with a special meaning:

Table 3: Sets

Sets	Description
[arn]	Returns a match where one of the specified characters (a, r, or n) are present
[a-n]	Returns a match for any lower case character, alphabetically between a and n
[^arn]	Returns a match for any character EXCEPT a, r, and n
[0123]	Returns a match where any of the specified digits (0, 1, 2, or 3) are present
[0-9]	Returns a match for any digit between 0 and 9
[0-5][0-9]	Returns a match for any two-digit numbers from 00 and 59
[a-zA-Z]	Returns a match for any character alphabetically between a and z, lower case OR upper case
[+]	In sets, +, *, ., |, (), $,{} has no special meaning, so [+] means: return a match for any + character in the string

Do It Yourself

Q. **Write a program using RegEx that will replace all the digits in a string with an exclamation (!) sign.**

Day 2: String Manipulation using RegEx

So, after successfully understanding, writing, and compiling our 1ˢᵗ program we are all set to move further.

Today, on Day 2 we will do some interesting operations on the string using RegEx. Beginning with our 1ˢᵗ program which was to replace any digits present in the string with an underscore, let's do the opposite operation now. That is, to replace (or substitute) non- digits with an underscore sign.

#Task 1 (Day 2): Our 2ⁿᵈ task is to **write a program that will replace all the non- digits in a string with a '_' sign?**

Referring to **Table 1** again, similar to \d which specifies digits, we have \D which specifies non-digits. It means that if in our 1ˢᵗ program if we replace \d with \D, our objective must be achieved. Let's check it out.

```
import re
pattern = re.compile(r"")
my_string = input("Enter a string: ")
pattern = re.compile(r"\D")
result = pattern.sub("_",my_string)
print(result)

Enter a string: tonystark123
_____123
```

It's working cool. The non-digits in the string are substituted by an underscore.

What about using Quantifiers?

```
import re
pattern = re.compile(r"")
my_string = input("Enter a string: ")
pattern = re.compile(r"\D+")
result = pattern.sub("_",my_string)
print(result)

Enter a string: stark123
_123
```

The quantifier '+' is working also in a similar manner like it was in 1st program.

We should try 1 more thing. Do non-digits mean everything except digits or it only means alphabets? What about any special character?

```
import re
pattern = re.compile(r"")
my_string = input("Enter a string: ")
pattern = re.compile(r"\D+")
result = pattern.sub("_",my_string)
print(result)

Enter a string: tony@123
_123
```

If we see, the special character @ is also substituted by an underscore. That's great. That's what non-digit means.

Like \d is equivalent to [0-9], \D is equivalent to [^0-9], where ^ sign can be 'treated' as **negation**, here. So, replacing \D with [^0-9] gives the same result.

```
import re
pattern = re.compile(r"")
my_string = input("Enter a string: ")
pattern = re.compile(r"[^0-9]+")
result = pattern.sub("$",my_string)
print(result)
```

```
Enter a string: 123tony456
123$456
```

Now, we are familiar with **\d** and **\D** along with the **sub** function. What if someone says to find out all the digits in the input string? We know that for digits we will use **\d**. To find all digits, RegEx gives a function called *findall*.

```
import re
my_string = input("Enter a string: ")
result = re.findall(r"\d",my_string)
print(result)
```

```
Enter a string: bond007
['0', '0', '7']
```

What this **3rd line of code** is doing? It's finding all the digits of the given input string and printing the result in form of a list. Also, I have done 1 more change to demonstrate only. I have not written that 2nd line which I stressed to be mandatory. And as said earlier, everything will work smoothly. It's simply a good practice.

What about Quantifier? Will it affect you in some way?

```
import re
my_string = input("Enter a string: ")
result = re.findall(r"\d+",my_string)
print(result)
```

```
Enter a string: bond007
['007']
```

So, the '+' has converted the list of 3 elements as 1 element, but we still know all the digits present in the string.

3.1 ^ and $

^, and, $ are boundaries. ^ marks the start and is also known as Hat, while $ marks the end of a regular expression. These are very handy syntax to play with.

Wait a while…

^ used earlier denoted negation. Then, here it is being mentioned as starting point of a regular expression. When used in square brackets [^ ...] it means *not*.

Let's do some programs to justify our statements.

#Task 2 (Day 2): **Write a program to verify the 1st letter of the input string is correct as it was entered.**

```
import re

my_str = "Bond! James Bond"
pattern = re.findall("^Bond", my_str)
if (pattern):
  print("Yes, the string starts with 'Bond'")
else:
  print("No match")
```

```
Yes, the string starts with 'Bond'
```

The input string entered was Bond as its 1st word. ^Bond is checking whether the 1st word is Bond or not. When **if** condition was executed after checking, the result was printed.

What if 1st word was not Bond and something else?

Say, the 1st word is James. Then, accordingly, else condition should be executed.

```
import re

my_str = "Bond! James Bond"
pattern = re.findall("^James", my_str)
if (pattern):
  print("Yes, the string starts with 'Bond'")
else:
  print("No match")
```

No match

Nice!!

Is it checking the 1st word or 1st letter? It's checking the 1st both. ^Bond or ^James is executing according to our desired answer here because of the 1st letter, i.e., B and J and as well as Bond and James. If we change the word but keep the 1st letter the same, it will not work.

```
import re

my_str = "Bond! James Bond"
pattern = re.findall("^Blond", my_str)
if (pattern):
  print("Yes, the string starts with 'Bond'")
else:
  print("No match")
```

No match

But if we check for 1st letter only then it will give the desired answer.

```
import re

my_str = "Bond! James Bond"
pattern = re.findall("^B", my_str)
if (pattern):
  print("Yes, the string starts with 'B'")
else:
  print("No match")
```

```
Yes, the string starts with 'B'
```

Let's clarify this with another example, but, by checking the last letter, i.e. using the $ sign.

#Task 3 (Day 2): **Write a program to verify the last letter of the input string is correct as it was entered.**

```
import re

my_str = "Bond! James Bond 007"
pattern = re.findall("7$", my_str)
if (pattern):
  print("Yes, the string ends with '007'")
else:
  print("No match")
```

```
Yes, the string ends with '007'
```

```
import re

my_str = "Bond! James Bond 007"
pattern = re.findall("007$", my_str)
if (pattern):
  print("Yes, the string ends with '007'")
else:
  print("No match")
```

```
Yes, the string ends with '007'
```

For checking the last letter, **$** sign is used. 007$ or 7$ has the same meaning. But 807$ will execute else loop.

```
import re

my_str = "Bond! James Bond 007"
pattern = re.findall("807$", my_str)
if (pattern):
  print("Yes, the string ends with '007'")
else:
  print("No match")
```

No match

Moving on, again referring to Table 1, let's check out another special sequence \A.

#Task 4 (Day 2): Write a program to verify the 1st letter of the input string is correct as it was entered, without using the ^ operator.

```
import re

my_str = "Patience is the key to success"
result = re.findall("\APatience", my_str)
print(result)
if (result):
  print("Yes, there is a match!")
else:
  print("No match")
```

['Patience']
Yes, there is a match!

So, \A will check for the entire 1st word and give the result accordingly. It is similar to using the ^ sign.

#Task 5 (Day 2): Write a program to search any given word of the input string and also verify its position.

Say the string entered is "**The truth is...I am Iron Man**". I have to find that if the word Iron exists in this string and also what is its position.

```
import re

my_str = "The truth is...I am Iron Man"
result = re.search("Iron", my_str)
print(result)
if (result):
    print("Yes, there is a match!")
else:
    print("No match")
```
```
<_sre.SRE_Match object; span=(20, 24), match='Iron'>
Yes, there is a match!
```

So, there is a match. Here, we introduced a new function *search* (see line 3 of the above code). It's searching for the given word in the input string.

Also, look at the output.

$$span=(20, 24), match='Iron'>$$

If you count, then it's observable that, after 20 positions (including spaces), the word Iron is starting and goes till the 24th position.

The *search ()* function searches the string for a match, and returns a Match object if there is a match.

If there is more than one match, only the first occurrence of the match will be returned:

```
import re

my_str = "The truth is...I am The Iron Man"
result = re.search("The", my_str)
print(result)
if (result):
   print("Yes, there is a match!")
else:
   print("No match")
```

```
<_sre.SRE_Match object; span=(0, 3), match='The'>
Yes, there is a match!
```

There are two The in the input string. But the search function will give the result of only the 1st matching it encountered.

If we see, **findall** and **search** are doing the same thing. So, what's the difference? Writing the above code using findall will give…what? Let's check:

```
import re

my_str = "The truth is...I am The Iron Man"
result = re.findall("The", my_str)
print(result)
if (result):
   print("Yes, there is a match!")
else:
   print("No match")
```

```
['The', 'The']
Yes, there is a match!
```

Wow!! So **findall** is giving all the same words. But it's not giving the span, while **search** is giving the 1st matched occurrence with span.

Moving forward towards another important function **split**

The **split ()** function returns a list where the string has been split at each match.

```
import re

my_str = "We are Venom"
result = re.split("\s", my_str)
print(result)

['We', 'are', 'Venom']
```

So, **split ()** simply creates a list. \s is splitting the string at each whitespace occurrence.

There is a special case with the **split ()** function which allows splitting the n words. Suppose I want to split 1st two words of my string and not the remaining. Then, it goes like this:

```
import re

my_str = "The name is Cable"
result = re.split("\s", my_str, 2)
print(result)

['The', 'name', 'is Cable']
```

Look at the 3rd line of code. There is a number '2', which indicates how many words to split. What if it becomes 1?

```
import re

my_str = "The name is Cable"
result = re.split("\s", my_str, 1)
print(result)

['The', 'name is Cable']
```

Only 1 word has split and the remaining words are combined as 1 word in the output list. Some variation in the **split ()** function will be seen later.

3.2 Match Object

A Match Object is an object containing information about the search and the result. There are some attributes related to **search** operation:

.span () returns a tuple containing the start-, and end positions of the match.

.string returns the string passed into the function

.group () returns the part of the string where there was a match (We will learn this function in detail on the last day of our course)

Before ending Day 2, let's do some tasks using these search function parameters.

#Task 6 (Day 2): **Write a program to search for an upper case character at the beginning of a word, and print its position.**

For example, the string is "**I am Iron Man**". The task is to find the position of, say, letter M of the word Man. What should be the approach?

1. Check for the 1st character of the string. For example, the 1st word here is not M. It's I. So, I can't use ^ or \A.
2. Referring to **Table 1** again. There are two special sequences \b and \w.
3. \b returns a match where the specified characters are at the beginning or the end of a word.
4. \w returns a match where the string contains any word characters
5. Finally, using .span () will do the job.

The final code will look like this:

```
import re

my_str = "I am Iron Man"
result = re.search(r"\bM\w+", my_str)
print(result.span())
```

(10, 13)

3rd line of code: \b will return a match where the specified characters are at the beginning (or at the end) of a word which is M (in this example) and \w will return the match where the string contains any word character. .span () returns a tuple containing the start-, and end positions of the match, i.e. (10, 13), in our example.

#Task 7 (Day 2): **Write a program to search for an upper case character at the beginning of a word, and print that complete word.**

For example, the string is "**I am Iron Man**". The task is to find the complete word of Man if my letter is, say, M.
Here, I will use .group () instead of .span ()

```
import re

my_str = "I am Iron Man"
result = re.search(r"\bM\w+", my_str)
print(result.group())
```

Man

#Task 8 (Day 2): **Write a program to search for the character at the beginning of a word, and print that complete word.**
Again, \b is useful for our needs.

```
import re
my_input = "Avengers"
dotsequence = re.search(r'\b[a-zA-Z]vengers', my_input)
print(dotsequence)
```

```
<_sre.SRE_Match object; span=(0, 8), match='Avengers'>
```

The code is simple. **\b** will check for the beginning part for lowercase or uppercase character which is written as **[a-zA-Z]**. When it finds *A*, it matches itself with the input string and prints the result. This format will be discussed in the next chapter in more detail.

.string will simply return the string given.

That concludes our Day 2.

Day 3: String Validations - I (Password Validation)

3.1 Validation

What does this word mean? How important validation is?

To begin with, one literal meaning of Validation is, *"**the action of checking or proving the validity or accuracy of something.**"*

Now the definition itself explains the significance of this word: "To check or prove the accuracy or validity or authenticity of something". The example says a password or User-ID or may be email-ID. In simple words, we can say that validation is to check whether the string input is in the correct (prescribed) form or not. **One thing to understand here is that string validation will only check that that string is in the correct format. It will not check whether the string itself is correct or not.**

Say, you are asked to *__make__* a password that is a combination of 4 words and 2 digits only. Let the password be: **mark40**. Using string validation you can check this. If you make a password, say, **mark411**, it's violating the validation rule. An error message will prompt. But string validation will not tell anything whether **mark40** is your password. That's the Database Management part. That's why I have underlined the word *__make.__* After making the password, the respective database must check whether the given password is yours or not.

So, on this big day (I mean Day 3, not any National Holiday), we are going to cover some very useful string validation operations using RegEx. Our final Task of Day 3 will be the following task:

Everybody has once (or many a time in fact), got chance to visit a site and make a password which prompts a message like this:

1. Your password must be at least 8 characters long.

2. Your password must contain at least 1 number and 1 special character.

3. Password must have 1st character in uppercase.

Write a program to code this out.

#Task 1 (Day 4): **Write a program to simply generate a password that consists of numbers and characters?** ☐

What should be our approach?

1. Enter a string

2. The string should contain digits. **\d** will help.

3. The string should contain non-digits. **\D** will help.

4. Steps 2 and 3 can be collectively said to be alpha-numeric. This we have not studied. Our Table 1 might help.

 5. Finally, print the result with some message.

The code goes like this:

```python
import re

pattern = re.compile(r'')
password = input('Enter a password:')
pattern = re.compile(r'\w')
result = pattern.match(password)
if (result):
    print('Valid Password. Your password is:',
        password)
else:
    print('Password Invalid')
```

1st two lines of code are mandatory.

3rd line of code will ask the user to enter the input string which is the password.

4th line of code: Referring to Table 1 we have another special sequence \w which is used for alphanumeric characters. So here we will use \w.

5th line of code will simply match the pattern generated in the 4th line with the input string and save the result in a variable called result. If the match is correct, **if** condition is executed otherwise the **else** condition will get   execute.
Let's run the code:

```
import re

pattern = re.compile(r'')
password = input('Enter a password:')
pattern = re.compile(r'\w')
result = pattern.match(password)
if (result):
    print('Valid Password. Your password is:',
        password)
else:
    print('Password Invalid')
```
```
Enter a password:stark
Valid Password. Your password is: stark
```

I gave the input string stark. It's a match. Let's analyze \w more. \w is equivalent to **[a-zA-Z0-9]**. What does this mean? We have seen this [a-zA-Z] in the last chapter. What if I write my password in all uppercase?

```
import re

pattern = re.compile(r'')
password = input('Enter a password:')
pattern = re.compile(r'\w')
result = pattern.match(password)
if (result):
    print('Valid Password. Your password is:',
        password)
else:
    print('Password Invalid')
```
```
Enter a password:STARK
Valid Password. Your password is: STARK
```

It's working. What if I give a password containing only digits?

```
import re

pattern = re.compile(r'')
password = input('Enter a password:')
pattern = re.compile(r'\w')
result = pattern.match(password)
if (result):
    print('Valid Password. Your password is:',
        password)
else:
    print('Password Invalid')
```
```
Enter a password:1234
Valid Password. Your password is: 1234
```

Again it worked. What if I write a password containing characters in upper and lower case and digits also?

```
import re

pattern = re.compile(r'')
password = input('Enter a password:')
pattern = re.compile(r'\w')
result = pattern.match(password)
if (result):
    print('Valid Password. Your password is:',
        password)
else:
    print('Password Invalid')
```
```
Enter a password:ToNyStARk911
Valid Password. Your password is: ToNyStARk911
```

This is also working cool. We have not played with the code at all. We have only changed the password. And every time it's working correctly. So, what is the power of \w? \w is a combination of lowercase characters [a-z], uppercase characters [A-Z] and numeric values [0-9]. And, collectively it is equivalent to [a-zA-Z0-9]. That's a powerful special sequence to use. What about any special character?

```python
import re

pattern = re.compile(r'')
password = input('Enter a password:')
pattern = re.compile(r'\w')
result = pattern.match(password)
if (result):
    print('Valid Password. Your password is:',
        password)
else:
    print('Password Invalid')
```
```
Enter a password:@#$%
Password Invalid
```

Oh!! Thank GOD!! Finally, the **else condition** got executed. I was wondering that **else conditional statement** is only consuming lines here.

It also means that \w do not support special characters. Nonetheless, it's the most powerful special sequence we have used till now. \w can not only substitute the independent need of \d and \D but also gives a scope of using \d and \D collectively. What about special characters now? If \w checks for everything which is alphanumeric, then, \W should check for everything which is not alphanumeric. Running the above code by replacing \w with \W, will give,

```
import re

pattern = re.compile(r'')
password = input('Enter a password:')
pattern = re.compile(r'\W')
result = pattern.match(password)
if (result):
    print('Valid Password. Your password is:',
        password)
else:
    print('Password Invalid')
```
```
Enter a password:@#$%
Valid Password. Your password is: @#$%
```

That's cool. Definitely, \w will play a role in our final task. \w is equivalent to [a-zA-Z0-9]. Can we replace \w with [a-zA-Z0-9]?

```
import re

pattern = re.compile(r'')
password = input('Enter a password:')
pattern = re.compile(r'[A-Za-z0-9]')
result = pattern.match(password)
if (result):
    print('Valid Password. Your password is:',
        password)
else:
    print('Password Invalid')
```
```
Enter a password:MarK41
Valid Password. Your password is: MarK41
```

Yup, we can replace it. Now, how to write special characters along with this?

```
import re

pattern = re.compile(r'')
password = input('Enter a password:')
pattern = re.compile(r'[A-Za-z0-9@#$%^&]')
result = pattern.match(password)
if (result):
    print('Valid Password. Your password is:',
        password)
else:
    print('Password Invalid')
```

Enter a password:Mark60@
Valid Password. Your password is: Mark60@

So, simply writing some special characters (or all, depending) along with [a-zA-Z0-9] will get the job done. Now, this is an important feature because you might have seen certain login pages which give the message, ". or _ not allowed". If we write [!@#$%^&*,/\?<>~] it will not allow . or _ in your password. This is the back-end part of how it is done.

Moving on, let's add one more parameter in Task 1. Our password must be of certain characters long.

#Task 2 (Day 4): **Write a program to simply generate a password that consists of numbers and characters and it should be at least 6 characters long?**

The approach should be the same as Task 1. Fortunately, we have studied \w by now. What about the length issue? What I have to do is to check the length of my input string. It must not go beyond 6 characters. Python provides a function called **len ()**. Nothing better than to code and see.

```
import re
pattern = re.compile(r'')

while True:
    my_str = input('Enter a password:')
    if (6>len(my_str)):
        print('Password must be of minimum 6 characters')

    elif re.match(r'[A-Za-z0-9@#$%^&]{6,}', my_str):
        pattern = re.compile(r'[A-Za-z0-9@#$%^&+=]{6,}')
        result = pattern.match(my_str)
        print('Valid Password. Your password is:',
         result)
        break
    else:
        print('Password Invalid')
```

```
Enter a password:mark60@12
Valid Password. Your password is: <re.Match object; span=(0, 9), match='mark60@12'>
```

Here, I have given a condition in the **if condition** that if the length of my input string is less than 6 then a message will be generated that Password must be at least 6 characters long. In the <u>**7th line of code**</u> I have used **{6, }.** This will check for the length of the password which starts from 6 to any range. *If condition* will check that password must be at least 6 characters long. But how long, **{6,}** will check.

Can I put a limit to the upper size of this length? Yes. Your password can be of specific length as well. Say, only characters long. Simply writing **{1, 6},**

```
import re
pattern = re.compile(r'')

while True:
    my_str = input('Enter a password:')
    if (len(my_str)<6):
        print('Password must be of minimum 6 characters')

    elif re.match(r'[A-Za-z0-9@#$%^&]{1,6}', my_str):
        pattern = re.compile(r'[A-Za-z0-9@#$%^&+=]{1,6}')
        result = pattern.match(my_str)
        print('Valid Password. Your password is:',
         result)
        break
    else:
        print('Password Invalid')
```

```
Enter a password:mark
Password must be of minimum 6 characters
Enter a password:mark41
Valid Password. Your password is: <re.Match object; span=(0, 6), match='mark41'
```

One caution!! When we use {1, 6}, any character written after 6th position
will be excluded.

```
import re
pattern = re.compile(r'')

while True:
    my_str = input('Enter a password:')
    if (len(my_str)<6):
        print('Password must be of minimum 6 characters')

    elif re.match(r'[A-Za-z0-9@#$%^&]{1,6}', my_str):
        pattern = re.compile(r'[A-Za-z0-9@#$%^&+=]{1,6}')
        result = pattern.match(my_str)
        print('Valid Password. Your password is:',
         result)
        break
    else:
        print('Password Invalid')
```

```
Enter a password:mark80@t
Valid Password. Your password is: <re.Match object; span=(0, 6), match='mark80'>
```

#Task 3 (Day 4): **Write a program to simply generate a password that consists of numbers and characters but there should be no special character present at any position?**

We can consider this task as a test case. We used \w and \W earlier. If you see, the task says that a password, say **Bond@007** should be considered invalid because a special character is present. It doesn't matter if the special character is at the beginning or is somewhere in-between the word or in the end. We'll modify the code slightly to look across the entire string for non-alphanumeric characters using '.*\W+'. Let's make a complete program which will summarize the use of \w and \W with quantifier '+'. We'll use the input password as **Bond@007** and will try different combinations of this. If the password entered is equal to the word **done,** then the while loop execution will stop.

```
import re
pattern = re.compile(r'')

while True:
    userpassword = input('Enter a password: ')
    if userpassword == 'done': break
    result = re.match(r'.*\W+',userpassword)
    if result:
        print('Invalid. Some special character is present')
    else:
        result = re.match(r'\w+',userpassword)
        print(f'{result.group()} is a valid password.')
```

OK. Let's check for the output.

```
Enter a password: Bond
Bond is a valid password.
Enter a password: bond
bond is a valid password.
Enter a password: Bond007
Bond007 is a valid password.
Enter a password: Bond@007
Invalid. Some special character is present
Enter a password: @Bond007
Invalid. Some special character is present
Enter a password: Bond007@
Invalid. Some special character is present
Enter a password: done
```

We can see that if the special character is present anywhere in the word, it is treated as invalid password.

Finally, after these tremendous warm-up exercises, we are ready to proceed with our final task of Day 4. Recalling it, the Task was:

1. Your password must be at least 8 characters long

2. Your password must contain at least 1 number and 1 special character.

3. **Password must have 1st character in uppercase**

```
import re
pattern = re.compile(r'')

while True:
    my_str = input('Enter a password:')
    if (8>len(my_str)):
        print('Password must be of minimum 8 characters')

    if re.search(r'[!@#$&]', my_str) is None:
        print('Password must have 1 special character')

    if re.search(r'\d', my_str) is None:
        print('Password must have 1 digit')

    if my_str and not my_str[0].isupper():
        print('First character must be a capital letter')

    elif re.match(r'[A-Za-z0-9@#$%^&]{8,}', my_str):
        pattern = re.compile(r'[A-Za-z0-9@#$%^&+=]{8,}')
        result = pattern.match(my_str)
        print('Valid Password. Your password is:',
         result)
        break
    else:
        print('Password Invalid')
```

It's the combination of all the above exercises which we just did. The new part is the **4th if condition**. It says that if the 1st character of the input string (written as [0]th position) is not in uppercase then prompt a message. Why this line is necessary? This is because we are using [a-zA-Z0-9]. It consists of uppercase characters as well. If accidentally someone writes the 1st character in uppercase then it's OK. But if not, then this condition will help.

```
Enter a password:mark60@avengers
First character must be a capital letter
Enter a password:Mark60@avengers
Valid Password. Your password is: <re.Match object; span=(0, 15), match='Mark60@avengers'>
```

Now I have a strong password with a capital letter, small letters, numbers, and special characters. This is how password validation is done on login pages.

One final shot: I made a strong password. But I got an intuition that while I was making my password, someone was peeping into my computer. What if when I type everything it appears in the form of dots so that only I know?

For this, Python provides a module known as **getpass ().getpass ()** prompts the user for a password without echoing. Only additional two lines are required.

1st line is to *import getpass*

2nd line is to write *getpass.getpass ("Enter the password: "),* instead of, *input ("Enter the password: ")*

```
import re
import getpass
pattern = re.compile(r'')

while True:
    my_str = getpass.getpass('Enter a password:')
    if (8>len(my_str)):
        print('Password must be of minimum 8 characters')
    if re.search(r'[!@#$&]', my_str) is None:
        print('Password must have 1 special character')
    if re.search(r'\d', my_str) is None:
        print('Password must have 1 digit')
    if my_str and not my_str[0].isupper():
        print('First character must be a capital letter')
    elif re.match(r'[A-Za-z0-9@#$%^&]{8,}', my_str):
        pattern = re.compile(r'[A-Za-z0-9@#$%^&+=]{8,}')
        result = pattern.match(my_str)
        print('Valid Password. Your password is:',
         result)
        break
    else:
        print('Password Invalid')

Enter a password: ········
```

getpass *()* is a built-in method to improve the security while typing itself. See the 2nd line and 5th line of code.

This brings to the closure of our Day 4 learning session of RegEx. Have a nice practice time ahead.

Day 4: String Validations - II (User ID Validation)

After Password Validation, another important validation is your Login ID/ Login Name/ User ID or User Name Validation. Usually, there are not many restrictions in making a User ID except a few. That's why I chose the Password Validation topic ahead of this topic. If you can make a password validatory code, the same can be applied for the user ID validatory code also. Still, let's make a common validatory code which we mostly see. The task goes like this:

#Task 1 (Day 4): **Write a validatory code to check a user ID that satisfies the following conditions:**

1. Only contains alphanumeric characters, *underscore,* and *dot*.
2. Underscore and dot can't be *next to each other* (e.g. abc_.def).
3. Underscore or dot can't be used multiple times *in a row* (e.g. abc__def / abc..def).
4. Underscore and dot can't be at the *end* or *start* of a username (e.g. _abc / abc_ / .abc / abc.)

This is the most general format we all see, almost in every login site. Let's try to sort it out. What should be the approach?

1. Only contains alphanumeric characters, an underscore and a dot. This we have studied on last day. Something like this might help: [a-zA-Z0-9._]

2. Underscore or dot must not follow each other. This is something that requires a thought process. For time being, it says [! . _], i.e., **not . _** (heights of non-technicality)
3. Step 2 will fulfill our 3rd requirement of Task as well.
4. Using ^ anchor can solve our 4th requirement.

Let's code it:

```
import re
pattern = re.compile(r"")

username = input("Enter a username: ")
pattern = re.compile(r"^[a-zA-Z0-9._]$")
result = pattern.match(username)
print(result)
if (result):
    print("Username Formation is Successful")
else:
    print("Invalid Username")
```

I have used anchor ^ to ensure that 1st letter must not be . or _. What should be the output?

```
Enter a username: tony_stark
None
Invalid Username
```

What!! Invalid. Why?

What should be the reason? I want some alphanumeric character followed by . or _ followed by another alphanumeric character. It means that I have to write (or add) two alphanumeric characters with . or _ in between. **Oh Yes!! I have to do this. ' | 'operator will help.**

```
import re
pattern = re.compile(r"")

username = input("Enter a username: ")
pattern = re.compile(r"^[a-zA-Z0-9._]|[a-zA-Z0-9]$")
result = pattern.match(username)
print(result)
if (result):
    print("Username Formation is Successful")
else:
    print("Invalid Username")
```

```
Enter a username: tony.stark
<_sre.SRE_Match object; span=(0, 1), match='t'>
Username Formation is Successful
```

Oh great!! The Pipe operator is working. I had to simply add (logic only, not literally) two alphanumeric characters. Moving on to another part, how to avoid successive use of **..** or __ or **._**? For this, RegEx provides an important concept known as *positive and negative look ahead*. Here, we have to deal with a negative look ahead whose syntax goes like this, **a [? ! b]**, which means *a not followed by b.* In our case, it will be **[._] [? ! ._]**. Read it as dot underscore not followed by dot underscore. Slightly modifying the code now,

```
import re
pattern = re.compile(r"")

username = input("Enter a username: ")
pattern = re.compile(r"^[a-zA-Z0-9]([._](?![._])|[a-zA-Z0-9])$")
result = pattern.match(username)
print(result)
if (result):
    print("Username Formation is Successful")
else:
    print("Invalid Username")
```

```
Enter a username: tony_.stark
None
Invalid Username
```

It's working now as expected. Let's check the code for some more combinations of outputs.

```
import re
pattern = re.compile(r"")

username = input("Enter a username: ")
pattern = re.compile(r"^[a-zA-Z0-9]([._](?![._])|[a-zA-Z0-9])$")
result = pattern.match(username)
print(result)
if (result):
    print("Username Formation is Successful")
else:
    print("Invalid Username")
```

```
Enter a username: tony..stark
None
Invalid Username
```

It's working. No two dots should be allowed.

```
import re
pattern = re.compile(r"")

username = input("Enter a username: ")
pattern = re.compile(r"^[a-zA-Z0-9]([._](?![._])|[a-zA-Z0-9])$")
result = pattern.match(username)
print(result)
if (result):
    print("Username Formation is Successful")
else:
    print("Invalid Username")
```

```
Enter a username: mark60@avengers
None
Invalid Username
```

It's working correctly. Only dot and underscore should be used. No other characters.

```
import re
pattern = re.compile(r"")

username = input("Enter a username: ")
pattern = re.compile(r"^[a-zA-Z0-9]([._](?![._])|[a-zA-Z0-9])$")
result = pattern.match(username)
print(result)
if (result):
    print("Username Formation is Successful")
else:
    print("Invalid Username")
```

```
Enter a username: _tony
None
Invalid Username
```

Working again as expected. 1st character can't be dot or underscore. So, it's working according to our needs. Another parameter one can insert in **Task 1** is the length of the user name. Say, I want the username to be 7 characters long but not more than 20 characters. Writing {7, 20} will do the desired job. Let's code it.

Task 2 (Day 4): **All that is written in Task 1 with the additional parameter of length. The length must be 7 characters long but not more than 20 characters.** We have to just write **{7, 20} [\w]** along with the running RegEx script of line 4.

```
import re
pattern = re.compile(r"")

username = input("Enter a username: ")
pattern = re.compile(r"^[\w]([._](?![._])|[\w]){7,20}[\w]$")
result = pattern.match(username)
print(result)
if (result):
    print("Username Formation is Successful")
else:
    print("Invalid Username")

Enter a username: tony_stark
<_sre.SRE_Match object; span=(0, 10), match='tony_stark'>
Username Formation is Successful
```

Before concluding, one security check: There are some innocent people like this person

<u>Innocent Face with Innocent Smile.</u>

While making his User ID and Password, he used the same name and password (*innocence or laziness?*). Now, this is a very dangerous situation.

This makes the intruder's work easier. Let's make a validation that prohibits this person to make User ID and Password the same. Let's help this person.

```
import re

pattern1 = re.compile(r"^[\w]([._](?![._])|[\w]){7,20}[\w]$")
pattern2 = re.compile(r"[A-Za-z0-9@#$%^&+=]{1,6}")

username = ""
password = ""

while not pattern1.match(username):
    username = input("Enter a username: ")

while not pattern2.match(password):
    password = input("Enter a password: ")
    if username == password:
        print("Username and Password cannot be same")
        password = ""

print("Username and Password created successfully")
```
```
Enter a username: tony_stark
Enter a password: tony_stark
Username and Password cannot be same
Enter a password: tony123
Username and Password created successfully
```

So, what I did is that I have compared the user-defined Username and Password. If both are equal then a message will prompt that Username and Password cannot be the same. The 1st while loop will ask the user to enter a username and it will be matched with pattern 1. Similarly, 2nd while loop will check for passwords and compare them with pattern 2. Then, the username and password will be compared. If they are equal, then, the user will be asked to enter a password according to the pattern 2 validation part. Also, one can insert or delete more characters in their pattern according to their need. (Do try and modify the length sequence as well. What will happen if both the username and the password have the length restriction of {1, 6} or {7, 20} or anything else?)

(The innocent man with the innocent face above is the co-author of this book. Currently, he is busy writing a non-technical blog whose link is ***my-perspectivez.blogspot.com.*** You can give it a read (*that's a promotion of his work by the way*). A little biography about him is provided in the ***About the Authors*** section.)

So, finally this way we have helped the innocent man. Let's conclude Day 4. Thank You.

Day 5: String Validation - III (Email ID Validation)

After Username and Password validation, Email ID is another important parameter to validate. Email ID is very important because almost all websites mail their information in your inbox (or spam), and, even you unsubscribe, the very 1st time when you are creating your ID on any login page, a verifying link is sent to your email. So, how to check whether the entered Email ID is in the correct format or not. That's why Email ID validation is required.

Let's begin and end our day with this small task of Email ID validation.

Task 1 (Day 5): **Write a program to validate an Email ID**

Quite a small Task lengthwise. But believe me; it's even simpler to code it down. What should be the algorithm?

1. An Email ID can begin with any character, i.e. alphanumeric or non-alphanumeric, i.e. abc or 123abc or #abc, etc.
2. An Email ID can have two or more parts, i.e. abc_def or abc.def and so on.
3. Let steps 1 and 2 above be collectively known as Part I of Email ID.
4. After Part 1, for our Part II, there must be a '@' symbol followed by mail server name. For example, abc@gmail or abc_def@msn, etc.
5. Finally, after mail server name, ' . ' sign followed by com or edu or org, etc.

6. One problem!! Sometimes the last part goes like this: .co.uk or .gov.in, i.e. a subdomain. Here we need two dots.

The algorithm gives an idea about how to proceed, but it also gives an idea that there can be numerous approaches to this solution. The problem is that there is no standard guideline to make, at least, the Part I of Email ID. It can be **cool.dude** or **$hunny_bunny** or anything casual or it can be absolute formal like a simple name. Fortunately, Part II is fixed. It has to be a company/organization/etc. name plus dot com/gov/edu/etc. (or with a subdomain).

Keeping this in mind, we will try to make a generalized solution for Part I and a standard solution for Part II. And again I stress this point, Part I can have many solution possibilities. And since you have learned quite a lot of RegEx by now, you can make your own now.

Let's code the standard part first:

```
import re

pattern = re.compile(r'')
user_login = input('Enter the IInd part of email ID:')
pattern = re.match(r'^@[a-zA-Z0-9]+(\.[a-zA-Z0-9]+)*(\.[a-zA-Z]{1,255})',
                   user_login)
if pattern == None:
    print('Invalid Email ID')
else:
    print(pattern)
```

4th Line of Code: It starts with a '@' sign, followed by **[a-zA-Z0-9]** which is alphanumeric characters sequence, **for example**, Gmail. **A-Z** is used because you might have noticed that while writing Email ID upper or lowercase does not matter. You can although be strict in making your validation code strict by using only **a-z**. One can also avoid writing **0-9** in this because I haven't seen numbers in this. Then, we have used **'.'** to write our domain name, again followed by **[a-zA-Z0-9],** which will give domain name, **say**, com or org, etc. Note that again we used **'.'** followed by yet another **[a-zA-Z0-9].** This will give scope for writing subdomains, like, *regexusingpython.wordpress.com.* {1, 255} provides us a scope to write a domain name of any length long (not infinite, but a long length which lies in this value of 1 to 255). One can also write {3, 6} or {2, 50} or anything depending upon their need. Also, I have used '*' in-place of '+'. The difference is that '* ' causes the resulting RegEx to match 0 or more repetitions of the preceding RegEx, as many repetitions as are possible. xy* will match 'x', 'xy', or 'x' followed by any number of 'y'. On the other hand, ' + ' causes the resulting RegEx to match 1 or more repetitions of the preceding RegEx. xy+ will match 'x' followed by any non-zero number of 'y'; it will not match just 'x'. Now, what does this mean by the way?

```
import re

pattern1 = re.findall(r'x\s*y', 'xy')
pattern2 = re.findall(r'x\s+y', 'xy')
pattern3 = re.findall(r'x\s*y', 'x y')
pattern4 = re.findall(r'x\s+y', 'x y')
print("* will give the result as", pattern1)
print("+ will give the result as", pattern2)
print("* will give the result as", pattern3)
print("+ will give the result as", pattern4)
```

```
* will give the result as ['xy']
+ will give the result as []
* will give the result as ['x y']
+ will give the result as ['x y']
```

The * matches 0 or more repetitions of the preceding RegEx, while + 1 or more repetitions of the preceding RegEx. The difference can be well understood if there are spaces. Looks quite easy. Checking for output now:

```
import re

pattern = re.compile(r'')
user_login = input('Enter the IInd part of email ID:')
pattern = re.match(r'^@[a-zA-Z0-9]+(\.[a-zA-Z0-9]+)*(\.[a-zA-Z]{1,255})',
                user_login)
if pattern == None:
    print('Invalid Email ID')
else:
    print(pattern)
```

```
Enter the IInd part of email ID:@gmail.com
<re.Match object; span=(0, 10), match='@gmail.com'>
```

```
import re

pattern = re.compile(r'')
user_login = input('Enter the IInd part of email ID:')
pattern = re.match(r'^@[a-zA-Z0-9]+(\.[a-zA-Z0-9]+)*(\.[a-zA-Z]{1,255})'
                   user_login)
if pattern == None:
    print('Invalid Email ID')
else:
    print(pattern)
```

```
Enter the IInd part of email ID:@gmail.co.uk
<re.Match object; span=(0, 12), match='@gmail.co.uk'>
```

So both domain and sub-domain parts are working correctly. This brings us to our Part I coding. Since this will be a long single line and writing and printing it in a single line will create a bad visual effect so here before writing the actual code I want to introduce the basic concept of line breaking. If I have a long sentence and I want to write it in multiple lines then we write it as follows,

```
a = 'Simplifying Regular Expression Using Python is a cool book to learn regular expression.
print(a)
```

```
Simplifying Regular Expression Using Python is a cool book to learn regular expression.
```

As you can see it's not eye candy. Using backslash (\ ) we can break this single line into multiple lines at the time of writing codes. The output will be in continuation although.

```
a = 'Simplifying Regular Expression'\
    'Using Python is a cool book to'\
    'learn regular expression.'
print(a)
```

Let's print the output.

```
a = 'Simplifying Regular Expression'\
    'Using Python is a cool book to'\
    'learn regular expression.'
print(a)
```
```
Simplifying Regular ExpressionUsing Python is a cool book tolearn regular expression.
```

Now moving on to our email coding part. Let us write this thing using the above backslash concept to make it readable.

```
import re

pattern = re.compile(r'')
user_login = input('Enter the email ID:')
pattern = re.match(r'^[_a-z0-9-]+(\.[_a-z0-9-]+)'\
                   '*@[a-zA-Z0-9]+(\.[a-zA-Z0-9]+)'\
                   '*(\.[a-zA-Z]{1,255})$',
                   user_login)
if pattern == None:
    print('Invalid Email ID')
else:
    print(pattern)
```

Again important line is **4th line of code**. The big line is having Part II as well which we wrote just above. Our concern is whatever is written before

@. It starts with [_a-zA-Z0-9-]. This means that our Part I can start with an alphanumeric character or with an underscore. This is followed by (\. [_a-zA-Z0-9]+), which means that we can have a name like bruce_wayne or bruce.wayne.

```
import re

pattern = re.compile(r'')
user_login = input('Enter the email ID:')
pattern = re.match(r'^[_a-z0-9-]+(\.[_a-z0-9-]+)'\
                    '*@[a-zA-Z0-9]+(\.[a-zA-Z0-9]+)'\
                    '*(\.[a-zA-Z]{1,255})$',
                 user_login)
if pattern == None:
    print('Invalid Email ID')
else:
    print(pattern)
```

```
Enter the email ID:tony_startk@avengers.com
<re.Match object; span=(0, 24), match='tony_startk@avengers.com'>
```

Check the output. It's working correctly. Now, why did earlier I say that this Part I is not standard? Because one can have anything in place of an underscore. I can put a $ sign or a # or nothing at all. I can put \W to allow any special character, like this,

```
import re

pattern = re.compile(r'')
user_login = input('Enter the email ID:')
pattern = re.match(r'^(\W[_a-z0-9-]+)*(\W[_a-z0-9-]+)'\
                    '*@[a-zA-Z0-9]+(\.[a-zA-Z0-9]+)'\
                    '*(\.[a-zA-Z]{1,255})$',
                user_login)
if pattern == None:
    print('Invalid Email ID')
else:
    print(pattern)
```
```
Enter the email ID:#tony_startk@avengers.com
<re.Match object; span=(0, 25), match='#tony_startk@avengers.com'>
```

Let's verify if the above code is also working for any email ID which starts
with non-special characters.

```
import re

pattern = re.compile(r'')
user_login = input('Enter the email ID:')
pattern = re.match(r'^(\W[_a-z0-9-]+)*(\W[_a-z0-9-]+)'\
                    '*@[a-zA-Z0-9]+(\.[a-zA-Z0-9]+)'\
                    '*(\.[a-zA-Z]{1,255})$', user_login)

if pattern == None:
    print('Invalid Email ID')
else:
    print(pattern)
```
```
Enter the email ID:tony@avengers.com
Invalid Email ID
```

OOPS. Invalid email ID. I want that the email ID can start from
alphanumeric **or** non-alphanumeric characters. So, let's put **or** operator
between the first \W and [_a-z0-9-].

```
import re

pattern = re.compile(r'')
user_login = input('Enter the email ID:')
pattern = re.match(r'^(\W|[_a-z0-9-]+)*(\W[_a-z0-9-]+)'\
                '*@[a-zA-Z0-9]+(\.[a-zA-Z0-9]+)'\
                '*(\.[a-zA-Z]{1,255})$', user_login)

if pattern == None:
    print('Invalid Email ID')
else:
    print(pattern)
```
```
Enter the email ID:tony@avengers.com
<re.Match object; span=(0, 17), match='tony@avengers.com'>
```

Now it's working correctly.

That's why writing an Email ID is a bit tricky. But it's easy once you understand the logic. You will find many ways to write an Email ID validation code. This one I find quite useful in almost all situations.

I hope, you also find it easy to learn and use and of course manipulate according to your need. That's it for Day 5. Have a nice time ahead.

Day 6: String Validation - IV (Miscellaneous Validation)

Today, we will learn some more validation or pattern matching which many websites include in their login page (or anywhere according to their need). These patterns include Date of Birth matching, PAN Card matching, matching of some social security numbers such as Aadhar Card, Validation of Credit or Debit Card Numbers, etc. Now, these are some sensitive information so before writing forward, I want to put a disclaimer here:

Disclaimer: Any number used in this book as PAN Card Number, Aadhar Card Number, or Debit Card Number is only for learning validation. It's imaginary in my knowledge. Still, if it's real and exists and is allotted to someone, it's a sheer coincidence.

Let's begin with validating Aadhar Card Number. Aadhar Card is a unique number issued to every citizen of India. It is used as an ID Proof, as an address proof and it's mandatory for opening the bank account. Therefore, validating Aadhar Card is very important.

#Task 1 (Day 6): **Write a program to validate the Aadhar Card Number.**

What should be the approach?

1. Enter Aadhar Card Number.
2. Aadhar Number is a 12 digit number, which is written as 3 sets of 4 digits separated by a ' - ' or ' / ' or simply space. **For example** 1234/5678/4321 or 1234-5678-4321. This we have studied.
3. 1st we have to check the length. **len ()** will help. The length of entered numbers should be 12.
4. **\d** will solve our purpose. We can write **\d{4}** to represent **digits 4 times**. Or we can also write **\d\d\d\d**.
5. Print the validation successful message if everything is correct or an error message if pattern matching fails.

```
import re

pattern = re.compile(r"")

num = input("Enter the 12 digit Aadhar Number:")
if len(num)==14:
    result = re.match(r"[\d]{4}-[\d]{4}-[\d]{4}",num)
    print("Aadhar Number is in correct format")
else:
    print("Please enter Aadhar Number in correct format")

Enter the 12 digit Aadhar Number:1234-5678-4321
Aadhar Number is in correct format
```

The code is self-explanatory as written in the algorithm above. The only important thing is the **4th line of the code**. Length is 14. 2 extra characters are required to denote **space**, ' - ' or '/'. Using length 12 will not allow inserting any character in between.

For the code to allow the string to find ' - ' or ' / ' or a space, and to ensure that the user only uses the same character in the division between the

2nd and 3rd group as was used between the 1st and 2nd group you can use a regex string like this

```
import re

pattern1 = re.compile(r'')

num = input('Enter the 12 digit Aadhar Number:')
if len(num) == 14:
    result = re.match(r'\d{4}(-| |/)\d{4}(\1)\d{4}', num)
    print('Aadhar Number is in the correct format')
else:
    print('Aadhar Number is not in the correct format')
```
```
Enter the 12 digit Aadhar Number:5565 8785 1828
Aadhar Number is in the correct format
```

I've replaced the first dash with a (-| |/), which should be read as **dash or space or slash**. This portion of the regex is in parentheses to both contain the expression and indicate that it is a group. When the regex executes it declare the valid character that was found here to be group 1. The second dash has been replaced by a (\1) which refers back to group 1 or more specifically the character that was found in the group 1 position. This allows the regex to find the three characters but only allows whatever character was found in the first position to be used in the second position.

#Task 2 (Day 6): **Write a program to validate the Date of Birth (DOB).**

DOB is another important parameter that is used in many login pages, such as, e-filling of the Income Tax Department. DOB validation is almost similar to Task 1 written above. The only difference is the length of digits. The format which is followed in India mostly is **dd-mm-yyyy**. **\d{2}-\d{2}-\d{4}** will solve our purpose. Also, the overall length has to be 10 (including spaces).

```
import re

pattern = re.compile(r"")

num = input("Enter the Date of Birth in dd-mm-yyyy format:")
if len(num)==10:
    result = re.match(r"[\d]{2}-[\d]{2}-[\d]{4}",num)
    print("Date of Birth is in correct format")
else:
    print("Please enter Date of Birth in correct format")
```
```
Enter the Date of Birth in dd-mm-yyyy format:16-09-1985
Date of Birth is in correct format
```

It's working correctly. Again, there can be many formats, depending on country to country and website to website. We can have mm-dd-yyyy or mm-dd-yy. Accordingly, **5th line of code** can change. Moving to another task, let's validate PAN Card.

#Task 3 (Day 6): **Write a program to validate the PAN Card number.**

PAN Card is Personal Account Number Card. It's an important card required for filing taxes, opening an account, etc. Income Tax Department uses PAN Number as its login ID while logging in to their website. What should be our approach?

1. PAN number is a 10 digit number (without space) and includes alphanumeric characters.

2. 5 characters followed by 4 digits and 1 character at last.

3. The code has to be like the above code, except line 5, which can be written as **\D{5}\d{4}\D{1}**. **\D** is used for non-digits as we have studied. Will it solve our purpose?

4. Also, we have to check that it starts and ends with a non-digit character. Anchors **^** and **$** will help.

```
import re

pattern = re.compile(r"")

num = input("Enter your PAN Card Number:")
if len(num)==10:
    result = re.match(r"^[\D]{5}[\d]{4}[\D]$",num)
    print("PAN Card Number entered is in correct format")
else:
    print("Please enter PAN Card Number in correct format")

Enter your PAN Card Number:ABCDE1234F
PAN Card Number entered is in correct format
```

We can also write **[A-Z]** in place of **\D**. Both have the same meaning. In fact, **[A-Z]** is a better approach because PAN is generally written in uppercase and **\D** supports both upper and lower case.

```
import re

pattern = re.compile(r"")

num = input("Enter your PAN Card Number:")
if len(num)==10:
    result = re.match(r"^[\D]{5}[\d]{4}[\D]$",num)
    print("PAN Card Number entered is in correct format")
else:
    print("Please enter PAN Card Number in correct format")
```

```
Enter your PAN Card Number:abcde1234f
PAN Card Number entered is in correct format
```

Checking for [**A-Z**],

```
import re

pattern = re.compile(r"")

num = input("Enter your PAN Card Number:")
if len(num)==10:
    result = re.match(r"^[A-Z]{5}[\d]{4}[A-Z]$",num)
    print("PAN Card Number entered is in correct format")
else:
    print("Please enter PAN Card Number in correct format")
```

```
Enter your PAN Card Number:ABCDE1234F
PAN Card Number entered is in correct format
```

This brings us to final task of the Day 6. Validating a Debit Card or Credit Card Number. These are generally used by merchandise websites where you have to enter your card number to make payments.

#Task 4 (Day 6): **Write a program to validate the Debit Card Number.**

The task is exactly similar to today's Task 1. There are 16 digits usually in a debit or credit card (in India at least), arranged in 4 sets of 4 digits separated by space. I think we can easily do this one.

```
import re

pattern = re.compile(r"")

num = input("Enter your Debit Card Number:")
if len(num)==19:
    result = re.match(r"[\d]{4}/[\d]{4}/[\d]{4}/[\d]{4}",num)
    print("Debit Card Number entered is in correct format")
else:
    print("Please enter Debit Card Number in correct format")

Enter your Debit Card Number:1234/4321/1234/4321
Debit Card Number entered is in correct format
```

There are 16 digits and 3 positions are required to insert any form of separator, either / or - or **space**. So, the length of entered number has to be 19. One final run of code by inserting space,

```
import re

pattern = re.compile(r"")

num = input("Enter your Debit Card Number:")
if len(num)==19:
    result = re.match(r"[\d]{4}\s[\d]{4}\s[\d]{4}\s[\d]{4}",num)
    print("Debit Card Number entered is in correct format")
else:
    print("Please enter Debit Card Number in correct format")

Enter your Debit Card Number:1234 4321 1234 4321
Debit Card Number entered is in correct format
```

\s is used to insert spaces in between two consecutive characters. Here, **\d{4}\s\d{4}** will allow the user to separate the 4th and 5th characters with a space while entering the card number. This is important to know because simply writing *\d (space) \d* will not let you insert space, like *\d-\d* or *\d /* *\d* let you insert - or /.

So, today we learned a few miscellaneous validation codes which are (and are not sometimes) essential. This concludes our Day 6 also. Thank You.

Q. Write a program to validate the IP Number.

Day 7: What Else?

So, after a long week, we have finally reached the conclusive day with the final question, What Else? Besides performing so many validations what else do regular expressions do? We have seen some string manipulation in chapter 3 earlier. Let's see some more operations which can be performed using RegEx.

#Task 1(Day 7): **Split the given string to form a list.**

The problem statement says that from a given string I have to find out all the words and, make a list. We simply have to check for spaces. What should be the approach? It's simple: **\s** will do the job. RegEx provides a function called split. This function has a literal meaning. It splits.

```
import re
my_str = input("Enter your string:")
pattern1 = re.split(r"\s",my_str)
pattern2 = re.split(r"s",my_str)
print("Using \s will give the result as",pattern1)
print("Using s will give the result as",pattern2)
```
```
Enter your string:RegEx using python is fun
Using \s will give the result as ['RegEx', 'using', 'python', 'is', 'fun'
]
Using s will give the result as ['RegEx u', 'ing python i', ' fun']
```

What if we don't use \? Using only *s* will treat *s* like a normal alphabet and not a special character. Check the output above.

#Task 2(Day 7): **This is an important task. Say, I have a file…a big file in notepad or a doc file. Along with some data, it also contains numerous email IDs. I have to extract all email IDs. That's the task: to extract all email IDs.**

```
import re

my_file = 'Post your queries at abhisheksingh@ggits.org or zohaibhasan@ggits.org'
email_list = re.findall(r'\S+@\S+', my_file)
print('The email IDs are:', email_list)
The email IDs are: ['abhisheksingh@ggits.org', 'zohaibhasan@ggits.org']
```

The solution is very simple. The email ID format is **a@b**. We have to match non-whitespace characters joined by @. For this \S (**refer to Table 1**) will be used. '+' is used to repeat a character one or more times. The syntax will go like this \S+@\S+. **findall** is used to find the pattern matching the format \S+@S+ in the input file. Other than this format, all other formats will be excluded. Check out the output of the above code.

#Task 3(Day 7): **From a given email ID in the input string determine the username and hostname.**

This is a new task and it introduces a new function called **group ()**. The **group ()** function allows extracting specific parts of the matching text by checking the normal parenthesis in the regular expression, and executing what is inside the ( ) parenthesis. **pattern.group ( )** gives the whole match while **pattern.group (I)** gives the Ith part. Let's code it

```
import re
my_str = input("Enter the string:")
match = re.search(r"([\w.-]+)@([\w.-]+)",my_str)
if match:
    print("The email ID present in the input string is:",match.group())
    print("The username is:",match.group(1))
    print("The hostname is:",match.group(2))
else:
    print("No or invalid email ID is present")
```

```
Enter the string:The email ID is abc@xyz.com
The email ID present in the input string is: abc@xyz.com
The username is: abc
The hostname is: xyz.com
```

The email ID has two parts. 1st before @ and 2nd after @. **group (1)** will check for the parenthesis before @ which is the username. Similarly, group **(2)** will check for the 2nd parenthesis, which is after @ and is the hostname. group () will give the complete email ID. One important thing to remember is the format of the email ID chosen. Here, it's simple. If one chose some complex email ID not supported by this RegEx, then, despite the correct code one can land up with an error. Say, my email ID is #abc$@xyz.com, above code will not run. Why? Because the given RegEx does not support such a complex username. Accordingly, one can change the RegEx to support a complex structure also. Fortunately, we have learned in email ID validation.

#Task 4 (Day 7): From a given input string determine the longest word in the string.

Now, this is a traditional strings question. The algorithm is also very easy.

1. Check for the words character by character, i.e., non-whitespace characters. RegEx provides us with \S+.

2. Check for the length of the word.

3. Define a variable, say, which will give the maximum length of the word.

4. If the length of the word is equal to the maximum length of the word then it is the maximum word length present in the input string.

```python
import re
my_str = input("Enter the string: ")
my_str = re.findall(r'\S+',my_str)
max_len = max(len(word)for word in my_str)
print("The maximum length of word in sentence is",max_len)
for word in my_str:
    if len(word)==max_len:
        print("The longest word in sentence is",word)
```

```
Enter the string: Learning RegEx is cool
The maximum length of word in sentence is 8
The longest word in sentence is Learning
```

This brings us to the end of our course. In these 7 days, we have equipped ourselves with knowledge of a powerful tool known as Regular Expression. Of course, this is not the end. It's simply The Beginning. There are numerous more applications, but, those applications involve these basics only. With some self-practice, you can master the method. Although I have taken immense care in writing these codes and content, still feel free to suggest to me anything which you feel can improve my work. Thank You for reading this book.

About the Authors

Abhishek Singh did his Bachelor of Engineering in Electronics and Communication Engineering in 2009 from Gyan Ganga Institute of Technology and Sciences, Jabalpur, Madhya Pradesh, and M. Tech in Embedded System and VLSI Design in 2012 from the same institute. Presently, he is Assistant Professor in Global Nature Care Sangathan Group of Institutions, Jabalpur. He is editor in python.wiki.org, blogger, You Tuber, and medium.com writer. He has written Python Programming Universe ver. 3.8, a science fiction 'The Z- Transform' and a murder mystery 'The Imperfect Murder'. All these books are available on Amazon.

Zohaib Hasan did his Bachelor of Engineering in Electronics and Communication Engineering in 2008 from Guru Ramdas Khalsa Institute of Science and Technology, Jabalpur, Madhya Pradesh and M. Tech in Networking and Communication from Indian Institute of Information and Technology, Bangalore in 2010. Presently, he is Assistant Professor in Global Nature Care Sangathan Group of Institutions, Jabalpur. He has a teaching experience of more than 10 years and industrial experience of 1 year. His area of interest includes Antenna Design, Electromagnetic Theory, Microwave Engineering, C, and Java programming.

www.ingramcontent.com/pod-product-compliance
Lightning Source LLC
Chambersburg PA
CBHW071029050326
40689CB00014B/3577